T0072502

Watercolor Rat

joan cofrancesco

authorHOUSE®

AuthorHouse™
1663 Liberty Drive
Bloomington, IN 47403
www.authorhouse.com
Phone: 1 (800) 839-8640

Published by AuthorHouse 07/20/2017

ISBN: 978-1-5462-0141-0 (sc)
ISBN: 978-1-5462-0142-7 (e)

Print information available on the last page.

"All that a man has to say or do that can possibly concern mankind is in some shape or other to tell the story of his love—to sing, and, if he is fortunate and keeps alive, he will be forever in love."

--h.d. thoreau

listening to
laura nyro
it's gonna take a miracle
a soft rain
hitting the roof
as i come

december snow
wiping red lipstick
from sake cup

i am a sane person
who hears voices
calling me away
from enchanted evenings—
i ignore them

drinking turkish coffee
listening to lennon
than having sex
on the road

logs on the fire
merlot in the glass
and thoughts about you

muse in a leather jacket
gold chain high top sneakers
please give me a break!

bring me
myrrh
frankincense
and gold
and i will take you in my arms

you remind me
of an egyptian scarab
in the metropolitan
a dung beetle
to worship

i drink coffee
in the piazza
not knowing
who i am

i write about moons
frogs and wine
like an old japanese poet
except for the lesbian sex

moon above
the vineyards
in the finger lakes
makes me want more wine

i'm in eldergarten
i take a crayon
and make a black cat
wearing red sneakers

blaudelaire's
hashish
hallucinations:
nude women
in clouds

my hands are purple
from picking mulberries
what colors are my insides

womens rights
i should be putting on
my pink hat and protesting
but instead
i'm wondering how the hash brownies
in the oven will taste
and if i'll be able
to stop eating them

to reach enlightment
you must get rid of
reaching for enlightment

crickets
chirping all night
i chant
a mountain poem

i have been clinging to
sitting by my open window
with pen and rice paper
detach
let go of things

i retire into
my second childhood
drink rain
go to fireworks
have a sleepover
watch cartoons
nap
then get dirty all over

fat orange moon
above us as we walked
i remember you love

ghosts under ice
at the erie canal
bass cooking in bordeaux

boogie til 2 am
drink smoke pot
fuck all night
sleep til noon
get up
boogie til 2 am

i'm in love
with used books
and old cities
but i hate
bathing alone

reading yeats' poems
for maud
as your naked thighs rub
against mine
in bed

half-drunk
outskirts of paris
ignoring ghosts of
proust and verlaine

night skiing
under the moon
a sip of your brandy
to warm me
then we're off thru pines
skis sparking and hissing
in the shadows

goat's beard
black steel
ice
powerlines
snowbanks
whiskey and walleyes
upstate new york

sipping chardonnay
watching the stars all night
escaping my past lives

i had a dream
4 green men
a voice said
they are here for you
i flew away
like a feeding family of finches

pen scrapes
rice paper
cat scratches
rug

hours skiing
down paths of powder
steak and scotch to come

ski cabin winter
luc ponty's electric violins
blazing
by the woodstove
skiers flying by the window
in their blue and red down
muscles of asses twisting by
in black tight stretch pants

reading henry miller
by candlelight
re-learning
how to make love

dinner
brandy and bullheads
sake and salmon
talk of whitman's
cosmic consciousness
hemingway's love of cats
as rain pours all night

the great battles behind me
i can live
sleep late
plant tomatoes
eat and read
japanese poetry

cat at rest
paws folded in
mandarin position

i see his muse
marie-therese
i stay all afternoon
museum
and take in the show
each painting lit by her yellow hair

beat book store
in boulder
picture of kerouac
holding his cat

i see baudelaire's grave
the flowers by it
not evil
and the cats
gentle

tarot for america

the devil is
covered by the 9 of cups
the emperor sits on his throne
smirking
the bridge that joins them
is the whole world

nude
in dresses
in bathing suits
jacqueline
marie-therese
francoise
picasso
out of his mind

take off
the leopard underwear
spread your lips
while i light
candles and incense

for me
it's always saturday night
you in your kangol hat
sweeping your long brown hair
out of your face
cigarette
between your thick lips

rimbaud
saw
boys jiggle too
as they walk

black lace panties lying
on my hardwood floor
black cat sitting beside them
i slice myself
a piece of black forest cake

self-assembly
black cat sitting
in my lap

loved women hated women
never forgave apollinaire
insulted gertrude
painted painted
never visited america
and made blue famous

you again
after all these years
sitting naked
at my desk
wearing only my blue
ny yankees cap
and thumbing thru my poems
you never go away

i had smoked 2 joints in the ladies room
she had soft dark sicilian skin
breasts like sophia's
kisses of chianti
oh what a tarantella!

beautiful girl
rushing home from work
down 65th st.
in the snowy evening
i'll never get to run my
hand through her
long brown hair
while she reads my poems
cake and never eat it

on the train
your long fingers tease
my breasts
as we pass barns
with crows
powerlines twisting thru pines

bly poetry book on the floor
calculus on the bed
i wanted to study
but i was always distracted
i'd read for 30 minutes
then make love to you

executive orders

this is how the world will go
everyone will drive chryslers
walls will be built
no more gay marriage
or abortion
2+2=5

when you call for me
i come running
like our orange cat
in heat
i split your kindling
then rub your feet

trumansburg 1974

mike getting a joint
out of his backpack
you by the dog
laughing
or was it the waterfall
mary by the stream
everything
free and easy

woke in your arms
kissed your cheek
in a chagall

brooklyn
hooded sweatshirts
pass out pot
turbaned cab drivers
drive past

listening to bach
reading joyce
with my horney cat
colette
and my depressed cat
sylvia

snow
pine trees
my hand
playing
your long hair

a page of kerouac in paris
where to travel?
everywhere

old sheet music
from a used bookstore
great for my collage

Modern
see
milton avery's
yellow cow

the ghosts swirl
in the wind
the cats just stare
and bristle out

you stroll past
my window
with your dog—
i feel that leash

i wake up
on the floor
next to an empty

finger beads
mumble hail marys
amazing grace
on the organ
priest gives communion
altar boys ogle
girls in tight jeans

life
i thought
you loved me

you took off
your earrings
one a dog
one a bone
and put them
on my bedside table
later
we knocked them off

i chant to
buddha
using stars
as beads

you wear small
white skulls
around your neck
talk about music

i wake and hear
one true thing
rain on the roof

my jeans my cat
my everyday life
perfumes

picasso said
5 minutes to draw it
a lifetime
to prepare

some of my best friends
are found objects

the moment
i was taken
in our arms
snowstormy evening
on champs-elysses

she drank her coffee
ate a slice of toast
put on her denim jacket
without a look
and left

you feel
my longing
as i massage
your back

provincetown
a fellini movie

the plane
flying low
a shadow
shaped like
a huge cross
over the tower

men used to drive
chariots to the stars
all i have
is a yellow vw

gnostic book
next to rimbaud book
next to bly
oh my leaping brain

my hometown
the dead walk around
thinking they are alive

painting at the metropolitan
man so insignificant
next to kilamanjaro

may i be
a gargoyle
on top of notre dame
for eternity

piaf singing
in my wandering
paris head
black rain
i need a drink

you remind me
of monet's garden

acid
basho's frog
in my tub
under a 60,000-watt light

9/11

ash
papers
flesh
flying onto
a mr. softie
truck

you're in my afterlife
hanging with
hungry ghosts

black cat
crosses the moonlight snow
my trance

cats purring
zen masters
in the moment

cat purring
on the tv couch
next to me
i take a hit
and it's *the twilight zone*

awoke with my socks on frank parker

brown splatter
by the black phone

forgot the
blue wash pan

stuffed with a
worn t-shirt

before the
sound of rain

on mexican tiles

poem after vincent katz

she was a poet
she had lots of friends
i was one of her friends
she had some cats

john crossed
abbey rd
and married yoko
the world as one

monet's garden
forever
japanese bridge
and waterlilies

in my red flannel shirt
and black sweatpants
a working class
enlightenment

i retire finally
get to feel
like maynard g krebs

your black bra
hangs over my bedpost
your thighs
like madonna's

i never was
a ranting
electrifying
vietnam and suicide
poet
named saint geraud
but i love him

my beagle
can be blamed
for all of my farts

dark cathedral candles
a postcard from paris

char
in translation
on a table
in mcsorley's pub

ancestors lurking
to warn me
about life's various peaks

cold out
black cats
curled together
jasmine candle
burnt down

autumn
upstate ny
watching cows
from my tub

an elvis impersonator
looking more like a hound dog
asks me to dance
can't say no to royalty

smoking hashish
reciting rumi verses
crazy as my cat

roof leaks'
faucet drips
who cares
i'm reading cavafy

jim's grave
people smoking weed
drinking jack
listening to
light my fire

chagall's blue cat
stares out the window
at the eiffel tower

reading a book
of zen poetry
my cat purring

late afternoon
does my cat think
my snoring is
how i purr?

every starry night of mine
belongs to vincent

my black cat
licks rain
off the white chrysanthemums

van gogh painted
36 self portraits
i use words

a bottle of lourdes water
on the night table
beside a jesus paperweight
and whiskers from a black cat
hung over
did i sleep with
st. francis's granddaughter
last night?

at the white horse tavern
intellectuals and beer =
assholes

she sleeps satin
in my naked sheets

bukowski
sitting on
the lions of venice
takes a swig of beer
and farts

a man in a café
in montmartre
spicering up his life

in the university library
bukowski
teaching me

ithaca waterfall
talk about hanging out!

corso's drawings
in *mindfield*
are badass

one-eyed cat
by the coca cola sign
swishing his tail
in honor of my russian hat

a mugful of guinness
black as my cat
i am loving hearing
sweet jane

racing toward his end
monet keeps painting
waterlilies

overlooking the seine
empty coffee cup on the table
the voice of piaf

smell of new #2
sharpened pencils
the sight of graphite
makes me want to write

to watch you
shave your legs
after the shower
satisfaction

1970
it's raining napalm
while people eat
rice and fish

upstate ny winters
colorful bulky sweaters

smoking pot
in a café
in amsterdam
listening to *the white album*
it's like 45 years ago

above your nakedness
never touching down
just hovering
that aura

i need
to get rid of
these visions
and feelings
so i can write
poetry

found poem from notebooks of joan miro

print leaves, skeletons, fishbones, etc., on a plate like the prehistoric stones in the barcelona museum

inscribe magic signs on bones and wood

incise ordinary objects like wooden spoons, etc.

find out if you can work on an entire hide like the ones they use for making the wineskins the peasants take when they go out into the fields

pyrograph pumpkins, which have been painted with white tempera, and once they are drawn, add
a little color

don't paint canvases on white ground but paint a thick but fine smooth canvas with dark ochre it would be more magical

i will make my work emerge naturally, like the song of a bird or the music of mozart

provoke accidents drawings will draw themselves according to the laws of nature just as flowers bloom when the time is right

think of william blake when doing a self-portrait

always have the bible open when sculpting; that will give you a sense of grandeur and gestation of the world